EMILY CARR

At the Edge of the World

Jo Ellen Bogart

Illustrated by Maxwell Newhouse

Tundra Books

To my mother, Edrie

JEB

To my mother, Maxine

MN

Text copyright © 2003 by Jo Ellen Bogart
Illustrations copyright © 2003 by Maxwell Newhouse
Emily Carr art copyright © 2003 by the Vancouver Art Gallery, the National Gallery of Canada,
and the B.C. Archives

The publisher extends sincere appreciation to the Vancouver Art Gallery, the National Gallery of Canada,
and the B.C. Archives for permission to reproduce the paintings of Emily Carr.

Published in Canada by Tundra Books,
481 University Avenue, Toronto, Ontario M5G 2E9

Published in the United States by Tundra Books of Northern New York,
P.O. Box 1030, Plattsburgh, New York 12901

Library of Congress Control Number: 2002116673

National Library of Canada Cataloguing in Publication

Bogart, Jo Ellen, 1945-
     Emily Carr : at the edge of the world / Jo Ellen Bogart ; illustrated by Maxwell Newhouse.

ISBN 0-88776-640-4

1. Carr, Emily, 1871-1945– Juvenile literature. 2. Painters – Canada –
Biography–Juvenile literature. I. Newhouse, Maxwell II. Title.

ND249.C3B63 2003   j759.11   C2002-905842-2

We acknowledge the financial support of the Government of Canada through the Book Publishing
Industry Development Program (BPIDP) and that of the Government of Ontario through the Ontario
Media Development Corporation's Ontario Book Initiative. We further acknowledge the support of
the Canada Council for the Arts and the Ontario Arts Council for our publishing program.

Design: Blaine Herrmann
Printed in Hong Kong, China

1 2 3 4 5 6   08 07 06 05 04 03

It seemed as if Emily Carr was born at the edge of the world. In 1871, Victoria, British Columbia was an isolated place – a five-hour ferry ride to the mainland and thousands of miles to Canada's eastern cities.

Emily's British father, Richard Carr, had chosen Victoria for its beautiful natural setting, mild climate, good economic prospects, and very British flavor. He settled his family there, building a prosperous grocery business and a lovely house with English style gardens. The robust and lively Emily – her father's pet – loved playing with the animals in the cow yard, singing at the top of her voice and getting dirty. Emily's older sisters often scolded her for improper behavior, but she was allowed to explore the nearby countryside and beach she loved.

From an early age, Emily loved to draw. She even constructed a little easel for herself from cherry tree branches. Her father, recognizing her talent, arranged for art lessons. At the time, many young ladies painted pretty watercolor landscapes, but few thought of making art their life's work. Ladies were expected to marry and raise a family. Emily had other ideas.

Perhaps her father's support gave Emily the confidence to be her own person, but in her teenage years, her relationship with the stern and staid man soured. Emily resented his unquestioned authority and felt that no one in the family understood or appreciated her.

When Emily was just fourteen, her quiet and gentle mother died of tuberculosis. Two years later, her father passed away and her eldest sister, Edith, became the head of the household. Emily hated taking orders from Edith.

When two of Emily's friends traveled to Europe to study art, Emily asked to do the same. Edith said no. Emily went to the family guardian and begged him to allow her to attend an art college in San Francisco, California. To her delight, he gave his permission.

In her three years there, Emily learned the basics of art, found her independence, and loved being part of a group of happy students who shared her passion.

In 1893, Emily returned to Victoria and began to give children art lessons in her home. Her sisters complained of the noise and mess, so Emily converted the cow barn into a fine studio. The following year, she had her first art exhibit at the Victoria Fall Fair and signed her work *M. Emily Carr*, the M standing for Milly, her family nickname. Still dreaming of studying in Europe, she began to save for the trip.

Emily had often heard her father talk about the Native people he had met in his travels. As a child in Victoria, she had frequently seen Songhees, members of the Coast Salish. She was drawn to their simple life, close to nature.

In April 1899, Emily journeyed by boat to the western side of Vancouver Island. She and her sister Lizzie visited a missionary outpost on the Nootka Reserve in Ucluelet. The Native people found Emily friendly and amusing as she used gestures to communicate. They gave her the name Klee Wyck, which means laughing one. Emily sketched the people and their houses, but not the forest. She felt that the forest itself was too immense and forbidding to paint.

On the trip home, the boat's purser, William Paddon, fell deeply in love with Emily and soon proposed marriage. Emily refused. The love of her life was her art.

Ada and Louise Outside Cedar Canim's House, Ucluelet 1899

At the end of the summer, Emily finally sailed for England and enrolled in the Westminster School of Art, but the conservative school offered her no new ideas. She preferred sketching outdoors on holidays in the countryside. During her second year of study, William visited her in London, still pressing for marriage, but she sent him home rejected.

When Emily could no longer bear the crowded and dirty city, she headed to the southern seaside town of St. Ives. But the noise and glare of the seashore were too much for her, so she moved her work into the nearby Tregenna Wood. Here was a gentle place with ivy-draped trees and birdsong, and Emily embraced it.

Always worried that her art was not good enough, Emily drove herself to overwork. She began to stutter and limp, to suffer headaches and nausea. Doctors sent her to a sanatorium in Suffolk, where she spent fourteen unhappy months. Forbidden to paint, she wrote and sketched in a little notebook. Emily raised nests of songbirds in her room, lifting her spirits and those of the other patients.

Head of a Girl 1901–02

Feeling that she had made little progress during her five years abroad, Emily returned to Victoria, where she found a job drawing witty cartoons for a newspaper. She tried teaching art to ladies in Vancouver, but soon found that she preferred working with children. She loved taking her young students out to paint in the open air, at the waterfront or in Stanley Park.

Emily's interest in Native art kept growing. Soon after returning from England, she revisited Ucluelet. Then, in the summer of 1907, she and her sister Alice took a cruise to Alaska and visited Sitka on Baranof Island. Haida and Tlingit totem poles had been brought together as a display called Totem Walk. This was Emily's first exposure to Native monumental sculpture, with its human and animal characters carved from enormous tree trunks.

Afraid that this important part of Canada's heritage might soon be gone, Emily made it her mission to paint as many Native carvings as she could – a huge undertaking. One of her first trips took her to Alert Bay, where she painted Kwakiutl community houses, poles, and people.

Old People's Pow Wow Platform, Alert Bay 1908

Emily felt that her traditional use of watercolor could not capture her vivid western homeland, so she sailed for France with Alice, in search of a new way to paint. The Post-Impressionists there were painting with less realism and detail. One group, the Fauves or "wild beasts," used daubs of wildly bright, unmixed color. Emily was fascinated.

She took classes in Paris at the Académie Colarossi, but soon became ill again and traveled to Sweden to rest. When she returned, she studied with a modern English painter, Harry Phelan Gibb, in a small town outside Paris and then on the Brittany coast. Emily loved the tranquil countryside and its people. She spent long hours painting outdoors, accompanied by Josephine, the friendlier of her two parrots.

Switching to oil paints, Emily adopted the Post-Impressionist style. At last she was freed from strictly realistic painting. Before she went home, two of her works were shown in a Paris exhibit. The art world was beginning to open its doors to her.

Back in Vancouver in early 1912, Emily held a show of her new work. Some people praised the paintings, but many preferred her earlier, more traditional style. Their criticism stung.

My Bed, Somewhere in France 1911–12

Eager to get on with her mission, Emily and her sheepdog, Billie, set off on a six-week trip that took them to fifteen Native villages along the B.C. coast. They visited the Queen Charlotte Islands, now called Haida Gwaii, and boated far up the Nass and Skeena rivers to remote villages in the interior. Some parts of the trip were wretchedly hard, with biting insects, bad weather, rough seas, and lonely isolation. Some were made easier by staying with friends, relatives, and missionaries. The trip produced almost two hundred works. When she asked the government of British Columbia to buy them, officials told Emily that her works were too artistic to serve as an accurate record of Native culture.

Despite her disappointment, Emily got ready, at age forty-two, to launch her artistic career. In a rented hall in Vancouver, she displayed a large number of works from the previous fourteen years and gave two lectures on totem poles. The public's response, which mattered so much to Emily, was far less enthusiastic than she had hoped and left her bitter and defeated. She returned to Victoria with another plan.

Skidegate 1912

Emily built a small apartment house, which she called Hill House, on inherited Carr property. She hoped to live on the rent money and have time to paint. Unfortunately, she could not afford help, and spent much of her time looking after the tenants. She even rented out her studio and slept in the attic. There, on the underside of the roof boards, she painted a pair of spread-winged eagles, each with a row of frogs. They were her company.

Emily had always been a sensitive, even difficult, person, but her moods over the years grew darker. She hated the snobbishness and falseness, which she called sham, that she found in some of her tenants. In hard times, Emily's pets and garden were of great comfort. From childhood on, she had had many creatures that were like adored children. Emily thought that animals were never false and had that best of all qualities – loyalty.

Though disappointment and drudgery had distracted Emily from her life's passion, she did continue to paint a bit, mostly landscapes, and exhibit from time to time.

Arbutus Tree 1922

Hill House made little money, so Emily found other ways to pay the bills. She hooked rugs to sell and, in 1916, went to San Francisco and painted ballroom decorations. Back home again, she started raising Old English sheepdogs – unofficially called Bobtails – later switching to a smaller breed, the Belgian Griffon. Hoping to improve her writing skills and even sell some of her stories, Emily enrolled in a writing course.

In 1924, she started making pottery decorated with borrowed and adapted Native designs. She worried about borrowing, but felt driven by the need to make a living. Firing the pottery in her homemade kiln was hard and exacting work. Emily used a wicker baby carriage to transport the clay and to carry groceries or butcher's scraps for her kennel. Several dogs would accompany her on these outings, along with her Javanese monkey, Woo. Named for the sound she made, the frisky and sometimes troublesome little Woo wore dresses that Emily made for her.

Woo (date unstated)

Emily's behavior made her seem eccentric. As a young woman, she had shocked people in Victoria by smoking and by riding astride a horse instead of sidesaddle. During her years in Hill House, she hung chairs from the studio ceiling on ropes and pulleys. She lowered them only when needed and sometimes not at all for unwanted guests. And though Emily wore conventional clothes for social and business functions, for everyday wear she chose loose homemade smocks and tucked her hair into a hairnet.

Being different was part of how Emily defined herself as an artist. She focused on her art and was annoyed with anything that came between her and her painting. She sometimes scared off friends by being gruff, overly demanding, or self-absorbed. Her friendship with a Native woman, Sophie Frank, however, managed to last thirty years.

When Seattle artist Mark Tobey stayed at Hill House in 1924, he advised Emily to spend less time on her tenants and more on her art. He urged her to participate in a Seattle exhibition, where she received honorable mention. Encouraged, Emily began to exhibit regularly again.

Untitled (Self Portrait) 1924c–1925c

In September 1927, Eric Brown, director of the National Gallery of Canada in Ottawa, visited Emily's studio. The gallery was having a show called Exhibition of Canadian West Coast Art, Native and Modern. Brown was impressed with Emily's work and asked her to ship paintings, hooked rugs, and pottery. He even gave her a train ticket so she could attend.

On her way to Ottawa, Emily stopped in Toronto and met members of the famous Group of Seven. Seeing their work transformed her life. Emily was captivated by the paintings of Lawren Harris, with their almost heavenly quality of light. She later wrote in her journal: *Something has spoken to the very soul of me, wonderful, mighty, not of this world. Chords way down in my being have been touched.*

Lawren Harris became Emily's mentor and friend. They exchanged many letters over the years, speaking freely, artist to artist. He offered unfailing encouragement, telling her, "You are one of us." Acceptance by the Group gave her a new sense of belonging.

The exhibition was a huge success in Ottawa, Toronto, and Montreal and earned Emily much attention. A whole new chapter in her life was beginning.

House Posts, Tsatsinuchomi, B.C. 1912c

Emily returned from the East reenergized and began to paint. By summer, she set off with her tiny dog, Ginger Pop, on a six-week trip. She returned to the Nass and Skeena valleys and Haida Gwaii, and made it to Kitwancool for the first time. Conditions were awful, but Emily thrived on the challenge and produced many sketches.

Shortly afterwards, Mark Tobey gave a series of masters' classes in Emily's studio. She was intrigued by his Cubist style paintings, with flat planes and geometric shapes, and saw a connection between this modern art and the pared down forms in Native works. With the influence of Tobey and Harris, Emily's work was maturing, becoming more simplified, more dramatic, and more spiritual.

Emily's 1931 painting *Big Raven* recalls her rain-drenched 1912 visit to Cumshewa in Haida Gwaii and displays a mix of influences. The painting reveals a powerful image with a strong profile, and solid sculptural quality. The shafted light in the sky reflects a Cubist influence, unlike the flowing greenery.

Big Raven 1931

In 1930, Emily's success blossomed as her works were displayed in Victoria, Vancouver, Toronto, Ottawa, Seattle, and Washington, D.C. She made more painting trips to Native sites and traveled east again, visiting artist friends and galleries and meeting American artist Georgia O'Keefe.

As Lawren Harris had suggested, Emily moved away from Native themes and gave the forest a more prominent place in her art. She devised a technique for painting, using inexpensive white house paint tinted with artist's colors and thinned with gasoline. Painting quickly – with sweeping arm movements on large sheets of Manila paper – Emily captured the motion and rhythm she saw in nature. The fluidity of the technique was particularly well suited to light, clouds, and water.

Besides being cheap, these materials were light to carry and dried very quickly. Some oil on paper works served as sketches from which Emily later made oil on canvas paintings, while others stood as finished pieces. She also produced a large number of fine charcoal drawings and pencil sketches.

Young Pines and Sky 1931c–1935c

As Emily moved into the open space of clearings and the seashore, she came to see the sky as more than just a background for a painting – it came alive. Emily's skies pulsed with life, flowing and spinning in circles. She was finding, as Harris had, a strong connection between religion, art, and nature, and the sky had a godly presence.

In the painting *Scorned as Timber, Beloved of the Sky*, a tree, rejected as too spindly for good lumber, is left standing all alone against the feathered, shimmering sky. Even though Emily had achieved acclaim for her work by 1935, when the painting was created, she still felt the pain of rejection and always saw herself a loner, on the edge of society.

She felt a kinship with trees as fellow living things and had a sad name for the uncut ridges of wood that tear away when a tree is felled. She called them screamers.

Scorned as Timber, Beloved of the Sky 1935

From 1931 to 1942, Emily went on sketching trips twice a year, usually in May and September. She rented rooms in farmhouses and stayed in borrowed cottages, not too far from home. In 1933, she fulfilled a lifelong dream when she bought and equipped a camping trailer. She named it "The Elephant," but later compared it to a protective mother hen. There was just enough room inside for her to sleep, house her pets, and store her supplies. She cooked and painted outdoors. Though she was nervous to be alone at first, she came to relish the solitude. The four years she camped in her "tin hen" were some of her very happiest.

The Elephant was hauled by a truck and set up near a good place to paint, such as a hill overlooking a gravel pit. Emily often painted in parks and places where she could hear the traffic on the highway and people nearby, using small groves of trees as her models. Nevertheless, she was able to communicate the majesty and mystery of the great wild rainforest.

Above the Gravel Pit 1936–37

Throughout her life, Emily had written silly verses, little plays, long and personal letters to friends, and notes about her painting. What she called "wording" helped her understand a subject better and to express it in images.

In 1937, Emily had a heart attack. In weakened condition, she turned her unquenchable drive to create toward serious writing. In her own engaging style, she described her childhood, her creatures, her journeys, and her struggles to make a living and to gain acceptance for her work. She invented another Emily, called Small, who represented the child side of her personality.

Emily read her stories to her supportive women friends, but CBC regional director and former English professor Ira Dilworth became Emily's most helpful advisor, editor, and confidant. He showed some of her work to editors at Oxford University Press, who published it in 1941 as *Klee Wyck*. The book won the Governor General's Award and brought Emily instant fame. Her writings later filled six other books.

As Emily wrote of earlier times, she painted Native subjects once again. A 1912 painting of a Haida shark totem pole was reborn as the 1941 work *A Skidegate Pole*. The pole is shorter and bolder in the new work, nestled into the sweeping flow of its surroundings.

A Skidegate Pole 1941–42

At last Emily's work was being exhibited widely. *Indian Church, B.C.* received special acclaim when it was shown in 1938 at the Tate Gallery in London. Emily had several solo exhibitions at the Vancouver Art Gallery, and her work appeared for the first time in a commercial setting in 1944, in Max Stern's Dominion Gallery in Montreal.

Though Emily and her sisters had differences, they were faithful companions to each other through the years. In 1940, as Emily's health declined, she settled many of her pets into new homes and moved in with Alice. Emily continued to paint and write, even after several heart attacks and a stroke slowed her down.

All her life, Emily had craved approval, but when success did come, she had trouble accepting it. She feared that she would become too full of herself. However, as she lay in a nursing home near the house where she had been born, Emily was thrilled to receive good news. She was to be awarded an honorary degree of Doctor of Laws from the University of British Columbia. Sadly, with convocation just weeks away, in the spring of 1945, Emily died at the age of seventy-three.

Self-Portrait 1938—39

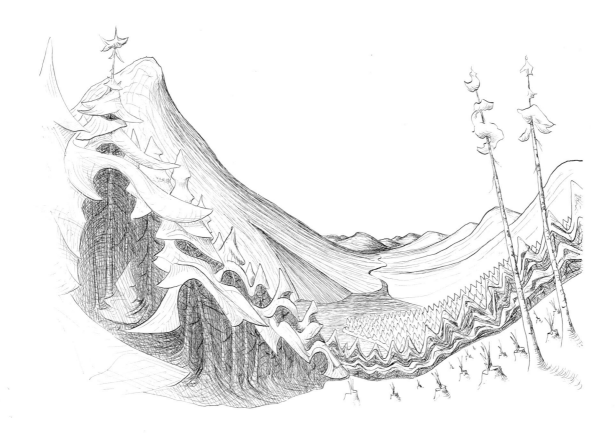

Emily Carr dreamed of being an artist and of finding her own way to paint her native land. With enormous energy and dedication, she explored art theory and technique. She developed a distinctive and personal artistic style, even in a social climate that did not nurture creative talent, especially in women. Though she drew inspiration from others, she relied, in the end, on her own vision. Emily poured all of her joy, sorrow, anger, and fear into her art. Through it, she expressed her belief in the vital life force in all things and through her writing, she let readers into the heart of one of Canada's best-loved and most respected artists – a woman who felt at one with her homeland.

I should like, when I am through with this body and my spirit released, to float up those wonderful mountain passes and ravines and feed on the silence and wonder – no fear, no bodily discomfort, just space and silence.

E.C.

Cedar Sanctuary 1942c

Timeline for Emily Carr

1871	Born December 13, the year B.C. joined Confederation
1890–1893	Attended California School of Design in San Francisco
1899	Visited Native community, Ucluelet, for the first time
1899–1904	Studied in England and spent fourteen months in a sanatorium
1907	Traveled to Sitka, Alaska and decided to paint Native carvings
1910–1911	Studied in France and changed her approach to art
1912	Traveled to Native settlements and created a large number of works
1913	Exhibited her art in Vancouver and gained little support
1927	Participated in the National Gallery show
1928	Took her second major trip to Native communities
1941–1944	Saw *Klee Wyck*, *The Book of Small*, and *The House of All Sorts* published
1945	Died March 2 in Victoria

Excerpts

The excerpts from Emily's writing that appear on pages 22 and 36 are journal entries from November 1927, as they appear in Emily Carr's *Hundreds and Thousands: The Journals of an Artist*.

Painting Sources

p. 7. *Ada and Louise Outside Cedar Canim's House, Ucluelet* 1899
    B.C. Archives pdp 02158

p. 9. *Head of a Girl* 1901–02
    B.C. Archives pdp 05923

p. 11. *Old People's Pow Wow Platform, Alert Bay* 1908
    B.C. Archives pdp 02159

p. 13. *My Bed, Somewhere in France* 1911–12
    B.C. Archives pdp 09004

p. 15. *Skidegate*, 1912, oil and card on board, 64.2 x 31.5 cm,
    Vancouver Art Gallery, Emily Carr Trust, VAG 42.3.75, Photo: Trevor Mills

p. 17. *Arbutus Tree*, 1922, oil on canvas, 46 x 36 cm,
    National Gallery of Canada, Ottawa, Thomas Gardiner Keir Bequest, 1990

p. 19. *Woo* date unstated
    B.C. Archives pdp 0603

p. 21. *Untitled (Self Portrait)*, 1924c–1925c, oil on paperboard, 39.4 x 44.9 cm,
    Vancouver Art Gallery, Emily Carr Trust, VAG 42.3.50, Photo: Trevor Mills

p. 23. *House Posts, Tsatsinuchomi, B.C.*, 1912c, watercolor over graphite on wove paper, 55.4 x 76.6 cm,
    National Gallery of Canada, Ottawa, purchased 1928

p. 25. *Big Raven*, 1931, oil on canvas, 87.3 x 114.4 cm,
    Vancouver Art Gallery, Emily Carr Trust, VAG 42.3.11, Photo: Trevor Mills

p. 27. *Young Pines and Sky*, 1931c–1935c, oil on paper, 89.6 x 58.7 cm,
    Vancouver Art Gallery, Emily Carr Trust, VAG 42.3.80, Photo: Trevor Mills

p. 29. *Scorned as Timber, Beloved of the Sky*, 1935, oil on canvas, 112.0 x 68.9 cm,
    Vancouver Art Gallery, Emily Carr Trust, VAG 42.3.15, Photo: Trevor Mills

p. 31. *Above the Gravel Pit*, 1936–37, oil on canvas, 77.2 x 102.3 cm,
   Vancouver Art Gallery, Emily Carr Trust, VAG 42.3.30, Photo: Trevor Mills
p. 33. *A Skidegate Pole*, 1941–42, oil on canvas, 87.0 x 76.5 cm,
   Vancouver Art Gallery, Emily Carr Trust, VAG 42.3.37, Photo: Trevor Mills
p. 35. *Self-Portrait*, 1938–39, oil on wove paper, mounted on plywood, 85.5 x 57.7 cm,
   National Gallery of Canada, Ottawa, gift of Peter Bronfman, 1990
p. 37. *Cedar Sanctuary*, 1942c, oil on paper, 91.5 x 61.0 cm,
   Vancouver Art Gallery, Emily Carr Trust, VAG 42.3.71, Photo: Trevor Mills

Bibliography

Blanchard, Paula. *The Life of Emily Carr*. Vancouver, Toronto: Douglas & McIntyre Ltd., 1987.

Carr, Emily. *Fresh Seeing: Two Addresses by Emily Carr*. Toronto: Clarke, Irwin & Company Ltd., 1972.

Carr, Emily. *Growing Pains: An Autobiography*. Toronto: Irwin Publishing Inc., 1946.

Carr, Emily. *Hundreds and Thousands: The Journals of an Artist*. Toronto: Irwin Publishing Inc., 1966.

Carr, Emily. *Klee Wyck*. Toronto: Irwin Publishing Inc., 1941.

Carr, Emily. *Pause: A Sketchbook*. Toronto: Clark, Irwin & Company Ltd., 1953.

Carr, Emily. *The Book of Small*. Toronto: Irwin Publishing Inc., 1942.

Carr, Emily. *The Heart of a Peacock*. Toronto: Oxford University Press, 1953.

Carr, Emily. *The House of All Sorts*. Toronto: Irwin Publishing Inc., 1944.

Crean, Susan. *The Laughing One: A Journey to Emily Carr*. Toronto: HarperFlamingoCanada, 2001.

Hembroff-Schleicher, Edythe. *M.E.: A Portrayal of Emily Carr*. Toronto: Clarke, Irwin & Company Ltd., 1969.

Hembroff-Schleicher, Edythe. *Emily: The Untold Story*. Saanichton, B.C. and Seattle: Hancock House, 1978.

Laurence, Robin. *Beloved Land: The World of Emily Carr*. Vancouver, Toronto: Douglas & McIntyre Ltd. and Seattle: University of Washington Press, 1996.

Neering, Rosemary. *Emily Carr* [Series-*The Canadians*]. Don Mills, Ontario: Fitzhenry & Whiteside, 1975.

Newlands, Anne. *Emily Carr: An Introduction to Her Life and Art*. Willowdale, Ontario: Firefly Books, 1996.

Pearson, Carol. *Emily Carr as I Knew Her*. Toronto: Clarke, Irwin & Company Ltd., 1954.

Shadbolt, Doris. *The Art of Emily Carr*. Toronto: Clarke, Irwin & Company Ltd. and Vancouver: Douglas & McIntyre Ltd., 1979.

Shadbolt, Doris. *Emily Carr*. Vancouver: Douglas & McIntyre Ltd., 1990.

Shadbolt, Doris. *Seven Journeys: The Sketchbooks of Emily Carr*. Vancouver, Toronto: Douglas & McIntyre Ltd., Seattle: University of Washington Press, 2001.

Tippet, Maria. *Emily Carr: A Biography*. Toronto: Stoddart Publishing Co., 1994.

Udall, Sharyn Rohlfsen. *Carr, O'Keefe, Kahlo: Places of Their Own*. New Haven and London: Yale University Press, 2000.